I WAS NOT BORN

I WAS NOT BORN
* * * * * *
julia cohen

NOEMI PRESS
LAS CRUCES, NEW MEXICO

Library of Congress Cataloging-in-Publication Data
Cohen, Julia.
 I was not born / by Julia Cohen.
    pages ; cm
 ISBN 978-1-934819-38-8 (alk. paper) -- ISBN 1-934819-
38-7 (alk. paper)
 1. Cohen, Julia. I. Title.
 PS3603.O366Z46 2013
 811'.6--dc23

                            2014028260

Design: Steve Halle
Cover Art: Noé Sendas

Published by Noemi Press, Inc. a nonprofit literary
organization. www.noemipress.org

TABLE OF CONTENTS

*****

******

your two irradiated wings
tremble with horror
for I will go
and bring you back the bloody evening
— Nelly Sachs

I know I want to awaken feeling
— Bernadette Mayer

I don't want to tell a story in memory
of someone
— Hélène Cixous

OF RECOVERY

Born in a deadlight? Stop teasing. Furnace full of patient stars. Here because I could not abandon love: coffee grounds, a box of opened cereal, cherry magnets. My bed unburdened by sex? To hold nothing against nothing. To hold nothing against.

The mental hospital takes: your shoes, your pens & pencils, your belt, your computer, your iPod, your cell phone, your wallet, your passport. For 10 days I keep N's brown wallet in the front pocket of my backpack. I take it out every night, hold it in my hands like a dead starling. I look through his IDs. I look to see if he left a note. Nope.

*

In 10 days I visit 19 times.
In 10 days we play 26 rounds of Scrabble.
In 10 days I tell almost no one.
In 10 days I bring N 17 meals.
In 10 days I cry at unexpected times.

In 10 days I do the laundry once so I can bring
N clean shirts. I bring the blue & white striped
collared shirt, it's his oldest & feels like worn
. pajamas.
In 10 days I wash the kitchen floor.
In 10 days I meet N's social worker, young &
chipper.
In 10 days I buy Clorox & scrub the bathroom.
Even the shower.
In 10 days I clean out the fridge. Shriveled peppers.
Salsa with a moldy lid.
In 10 days N's doctor asks me if I plan to stay with
N. Of course, I say.
In 10 days I vacuum the living room & hallway.
In 10 days I wait until the ninth to throw out N's
noose.

Light could not look. Inside my lung, the night.
I'm not dry land. Pages stuck together. So creep-
ing so day. Origin in simile. To subdue exploits. If
I thought fruit could impart, I would sample from
each seed. Untidy summer. Not afraid of child-
birth, afraid of sex *after* childbirth. Firstlings cling
or canter with help. A city named vengeance. In
tents, years blink out like seeds crushed from a
lemon. To make room by reduction: sink. This one
is taken? Bite of fig & ice-cream. A living. Out of
architecture, "Dibs."

*

Questions I can't ask: Why weren't you going to leave a note? What other methods of suicide did you consider? You were going to leave me without knowing how to cook collard greens & black-eyed peas? Without knowing how to make tofu-scramble? How many lies did you tell to sustain this deceit & what did they feel like? Who would identify your body? I once watched a TV show about how dogs won't accept the death of their owner unless they see/smell their owner's dead body. Otherwise they'll keep waiting at the door. I'd have asked permission from the police to take our dog with me to the morgue, to accept.

*

Remember: N reads to me in the bathtub.

*

Therapy Session #7:

J: Last week we were talking about external experiences that test or…within seconds transform how you conceive of yourself. But I felt like I walked away from the conversation not knowing what to do with that information. Like, letting outside things have such a strong effect. I guess? Reading a book about questioning gender when I was twelve & then letting that obsessively take over or dismantle my positioning of self...

Dr: That sounds like you're choosing for things to go that way, which is not quite the way it seems it went. But rather, it happened automatically. Jumping back to your first point, I don't know if we got to necessarily what we were supposed "to do" with it, but simply understand what happens. You described this experience at an all-girls school of stumbling upon a book that questioned sexual orientation, that first was a notion & then became a preoccupation, & then you weren't sure what you were supposed to hang onto about your own orientation.

J: Right, yes. I mean, that was one of those larger moments, but I feel like I have the tendency to obsess about many things &, not that there is a proper place to put something or that one should compartmentalize, but I feel like I don't know how to quiet some thoughts down. Not that events happen all the time where I lose track or feel destabilized from who I am, but rather I'm socially anxious. I'll send an email when I'm tired & feel like I got my thoughts wrong, & then if the person I sent it to doesn't get back to me right away, I'll obsessively think about how he or she could have misinterpreted it & I was accidentally offensive. Then three days later they do respond & are like, "you sounded tired in your email…" so I feel like there is some sort of concern about how other people understand you that's healthy & then in certain instances I can take it to this other level that's unproductive & time-consuming. That's where I get afraid in regards to how I'm considering my relationship with N. I can't decide whether I'm thinking about this situation most of the time because it's what any one would do if her relationship was in a complicated place, or if I'm contributing to my own unease by having this take over my thoughts.

*

My calamine-blitzed child. Lucky licit, I claim a mountain & adjoining lake I know what's lunging. Tetchy water or feeble soil. Like a future roof, the fingernail un-creases aluminum foil. My makeshift. My lifelike.

Will someone string cold lights through the tulips? Will someone close grief's atlas & ship the salt to bookend the night?

Someone briefly touches my shoulder while I sleep. Moat, moat, moat. My arm like a drawbridge lowers to the grasses, an unstamped postcard, slight glances through curt branches, grey trousers, the

hand-drawn airplane. Addresses. I pack myself
with milkweed & thistle. Season of what?

*

Remember: We write poems together by email, by
text message, on car rides, side by side at a bar.

*

The noose is longer than I thought it would. A sur-
prisingly smooth cord, soft & glossy like a doll's
braided hair.

For nine days I peek into N's backpack but don't
touch it. Standing by the blue dumpster to decide
whether to untie the noose, turn it back into knot-
less rope, or toss it in as quickly as possible. I'm
compelled to destroy the evidence, to leave usable
rope for those who pilfer our dumpster. N tells me
he looked up how to knot a noose on the internet. I
try to picture him researching this at Whole Foods
or the library where I go to play Scrabble & check
Facebook. He says the instructions were easy to
follow. The cord, bought locally at Ace Hardware.

Remember: N writes for me, "I will warm your
frozen hands / in my cold hands."

*

I cannot get warm. I cannot clip the syrup from the homespun tree. Cannot scrape the banquette into the baby swing. Blue leaves at last. I feel like I can feel.

Garden of babies? I planted the sun under the tongue of returns. A whimper winds the sound gears grind over. Foraged syntax. Who romps the ruins? To locate a glance in the forest, stride through the wild chives, the beehive swinging like a lantern. Honey & hiccups.

Success in stems. Success when the nod. Success after soft cashews. Success of preservation undermined by owners. Success of passing the feeling-baton! Outside of family. Holding your bear by the ear. To plump the scrawny feeling.

*

Therapy Session #7 Continued:

Dr: When you were describing that e-mail piece, it sounds like you were saying that not only do you worry about the other person's experience of you but that you spin out the worst-case scenario that the other person might have of you, to detailed & negative places. So it gets to be an involved process in your head.

J: Haha. Yes, more involved than the other person would ever give it time.

Dr: Right, they haven't been staying up at night. So that's also a process where not only are you obsessing about something & really taking up a lot of room in your head, but it's all stuff that's about your worries about other people's experiences.

J: Right.

Dr: Their experience of you. How your actions might affect their experiences of you. So these are ruminations of them, about you in relation to them. *In that sense, it's the thing that takes space away from your experience of you.*

J: That seems true. That doesn't sound good. It sounds not confident in how people...

Dr: Maybe it doesn't leave as much room for you to feel calm & comfortable.

J: I don't give myself that space...which is why I'm so anxious all the time!

Dr: Yes, & maybe it's a cycle that feeds itself. Obsessing about something makes it feel more important & central, which makes one feel like one should obsess about it.

J: Yes, I have these moments where I'm going through the same loop in my head that isn't getting me anywhere, where I can step back & tell myself this isn't productive & tell my brain to switch topics & get work done, or tell myself that there is no point in worrying about it, it's out of my hands, until someone actually responds to an email, until something external happens.

Dr: Say one more time what the piece is that you need to break the cycle.

J: I just remind myself of what's fairly obvious: obsessing about what's on my mind isn't going to get me anywhere because there is nothing I can do about how this other person is experiencing me. Or, well, I mean, I guess about that particular interaction. Or I tell myself that either way, it's not a big deal. Even the worst-case situation.

Dr: *The feeling you're having is disproportionate to the importance of the issue.*

J: That may be an uncomfortably accurate way to phrase it.

*

Thoughts fall into two categories. Faith: N naps & naps. I walk the dog, wash dishes, take out recycling. Don't cry in front of N. Instead, on the orange couch late at night or in the bathroom, while looking at myself in the mirror. To study the uncontrolled face. This is what it means to surprise yourself.

Unfaithful: when I divide our belongings in my mind. The nightstands, mine. Mattress, mine. The dishes & glasses, mine. Lamps, mine. Plants, mine. Trinkets & heirlooms, mine. CDs, his. Most of the records, his. 65% of the books, his. What of the book-doubles we threw out to merge our collections? Chapbooks, who knows. What of the artwork we bought together? Our dog?

*

Will someone skip over radio-regret on the crumbling wave? Slinking mischief cracks open an egg or loosens the pinecone. Wrapping-paper grip? A leveled statue releases.

I'm trying to be here. Here & not sad. Sometimes a coffee table equals endless. A feeling tramped into route.

Remember: N introduces me to black metal, to Levinas, to Hannah Weiner, to Alice Notley, to nutritional yeast.

*

The reveal: I miss two calls on the bus ride home. As I step off to meet him in the park with the dog, I return the calls to hear he can't make it. Can't? "Because I'm afraid I'm going to hurt myself." One stoplight, three intersections, the choking floral scent of a Laundromat. I run the six blocks home to find N deflating on the couch. A noose in his backpack, a mind full of suicide. 31 tall buildings in Denver. 89 local bus routes to jump in front of. I would write about anything else if I could think of something other than N.

*

Therapy Session #7 Continued:

J: I mean, in the first session or two we talked about how in sixth grade my best friend stopped speaking to me & then therefore all of my friends stopped speaking to me — how jolting & horrible it was.

Dr: Yes of course.

J: But that was based on nothing other then the whim of a twelve year old. There is an anxiety that comes from that which is: I can just be doing whatever I normally do & then all of a sudden my friends will decide they don't like me anymore. I totally know that's a sixth grade thing, but I see that anxiety rooted in situations like emails or miscommunications with friends. But I don't see that same thing when I think of my relationship with N. My anxiety is more about what's happening *to* our relationship with me in it, although clearly a lot of it is out of my control right now.

Dr: Is it possible that your relationship isn't exactly like the former dynamic because it's not so much that you think N is experiencing you negatively, but is related, perhaps to one of the byproducts of obsessing about how the other person experiences you: that there is very little space left for you to tune into your own experience of what's going on, because a lot of your energy is focused on the other person's experience. Could that be contributing to the anxiety in your relationship? What I mean is: if the process you find yourself stuck in is a process the results of which is you have had less space to feel clear about what you're really needing & wanting because your anxiety has caused you to focus more on the other person, then gathering data about what you want or need is not a process that is accessible or easy to you. In so far as that's true, in a relationship that's troubled, it could lead you to be quite anxious.

J: That sounds accurate. But when I view this relationship with N, I still feel like I'm very much concerned with how I'm feeling. But...maybe I'm just feeling things incorrectly! Ok, this is what I mean: if you're in a room with someone & you're trying to experience what that feels like, it should be a sense of community or connection, & I feel that community, but at the same time, thinking about how I'm feeling creates a distance. Like I'm no longer in the moment, I'm removed through thinking about my feelings. Does that make sense? I do feel like I spend a lot of time thinking about my feelings with N.

Dr: What are those feelings?

J: I feel sad a lot. I think a lot about the attachments that are missing right now, the camaraderie, the immediacy of attraction & spontaneity when both partners have energy. Or, sometimes it's the opposite: I'm happy & comfortable with this person, but then I also know that it's the same person who, when he's sad, can't physically hug me back. He just stands there with his arms at his side. Feeling happy but then knowing that there is all this other stuff swirling around it making any easy & comfortable moment more complicated.

Dr: So you're aware in a very clear way of what you need to feel good. But maybe part of the trickiness is that you just don't know what to make of this.

J: I might be having trouble with that in terms of the larger context. Part of it is that there are things in our relationship that make me sad but I don't know now how to express them to N because they center on N & where he is with himself, that really can't be rushed. He's working so hard & it's a slow process. But then there is the larger context of where I see/feel this thing & ask myself "what does this mean for our relationship?" I never have an answer. Or when I'm away from N the answer is I should probably get out. But when I'm with him, it seems like there is an immensity to fight for. Proximity, when I'm in the house surrounded by the life we've created together, much of it feels so good & positive. We want the same things for the future, although for a long time he hasn't believed that this future would come to him. But we care about the same friends, we want to write, to pursue academic jobs, to settle down & have kids and so on. But when I step away from that, I'm faced with the lack of camaraderie & the very clear reality that N does not yet know how to rely on anyone else to make himself feel better. He does not have the foundation to trust others to help him, & that's terrifying. And he's just learning how. He never learned those things, which is not his fault, but is also the situation we're both dealing with.

Dr: So why is it when you have distance you seem to feel more clear about what isn't okay about it?

*

Will someone kneed the hummingbird that despairs the tulip's chalice. Who in the leaf-lavished air will stick. Belly-ached into an album. Light lifts nothing. Forged opacity. Face.

Questions I can't ask: The week of your suicide-deadline, did fucking feel different? Did you think each time that week was the last? When you came home after failing, when we had sex, were you at all glad you'd failed to jump?

That Tuesday, N fingerbangs me in the middle of the day & I think, *maybe things are changing.* Thursday I walk with him into the mental ward.

Remember: He ties a red bandana around our dog's neck. N wrestles with the dog, lets the dog sleep between his legs, in his armpit, on his chest, when all I can do is curl up & read. Watching this playfulness makes me feel sure, warm.

*

Will someone continue the bleached rhythm of sand? Will someone impeach the lighthouse? And if I sink my lilac imitation in night's wool to vase grief? Call. No, *call.* Moss traps in a necklace clicking at the gate. Flashlight. Canteen. Instructions for temperature. & you, will you incline the lemon shore?

*

Meaning: One Act Play

(N slumps on an orange couch with hands covering face. J runs down the front steps & enters living room.)

J: What's going on?

N: I didn't buy my plane ticket to the conference.

J: Oh, well, that's okay. I bet we can still get you a redeye ticket if we look right now. Is that why you're upset?

N: I mean, I didn't buy a ticket because I didn't think I'd still be alive to attend the conference.

J: What? What do you mean?

*

Faith: Come on my tits. Come in my mouth. Come in my ass. Come on my ass. Come in my hair.

Come on my thighs. I am not absent in body. A new batch.

Unfaithful: When I think *I wish you had jumped*, I mean, this is uncertain, exhausting, I resent that I no longer imagine my own future. Silly halo, the opposite of slander. As if present. I have so much faith in N & so little I can do with it. My glasses like crossed arms in the crevasse of our hand-me-down mattress.

*

Mostly I think of N.

*

Bookshelves sway & N travels on airplanes with me to reduce the fear. He hate flannel, flaneurs, plaid. Anaconda coffee mug stumbling into laundry. Dirty keyboard. Scarf on the bedroom door handle, towel draped above like a Botticelli. The precision of parting wet hair. N wishes for a desk & then an annex to place it in. We don't need a bigger house, just more walls for the books.

Remember: I peel garlic while N prepares my favorite meal. Black metal growls on the warped record player.

Questions I can't ask: why didn't you break up with me when you decided to kill yourself? It seems selfish. Or, what does it mean that you didn't? To fight for hope?

Often I find N reading in the dark, he seems confused when I ask him, *should I should flip the light on?* We're surrounded by Stein, Zukofsky, Celan. Earphones cramp on the carpet.

*

Therapy Session #7 Continued:

J: Because what I love is immediately in front of me, & I have no distance to think about alternatives.

Dr: What do you make of that?

J: I don't know. The distance also makes it seem less real, like I would be losing less.

Dr: Why would it make less real what you're losing & more real what the bad times are?

J: That's just how it is! I'm not surrounded by the good stuff—ways of living together I can't imagine losing.

Dr: But you're also not surrounded by the bad stuff.

J: That's true. But the sadness is part of the daily life; it's not just something that happens when I'm away traveling. It happens when I'm sitting on a couch with him & watching a movie, knowing that there used to be more of this physical contact I don't get anymore. Feeling like we're talking about our day, but also not...I don't even know, something feels off. Partially shutdown or like we've forgotten how to latch onto each other, to look forward to that.

He's taking care of himself, but at the same time, able to be less present & to give less to me because of the consuming depression, & I'm afraid I'll adjust to this, expect less, and in turn give less myself. So that even when he's in a better emotional place, things will have irrecoverably changed. Despite this unceasing love.

*

Will someone tuck salt in the mailbox? Cursory lilacs. Will someone visit the false river, its spellbound child. A coast widowed into desert. Morning enemy? Take flattery out of response to sweep a face into a face. Descendant stars or marzipan feelings. Pangs, tambourine, rivals kidnap a keyboard to spool your note. Labor? Endemic split ends.

*

Remember: A prisoner, N, the offspring of religion.

*

On the 10th day I am afraid. Of N's release. The social worker asks if our house is empty of pills, alcohol, weapons. Yes, except for beer. I giggle. Maybe some cooking wine? N doesn't know I threw out the noose. Afraid of not knowing how to act with N. Will we have dinner & watch a movie? Which routines are okay & which hide us from each other? N, release to me N.

*

Hush little humming humming hummingbird.

*

I thought to adopt a second dog when my first child could handle the feeding & walking. Now I don't know when that will be. I had thought within the decade. To lose this projection, a hallway full of splintered frames. Familial hologram.

To recover your wallet?
To recover trust?
To uncover a terrified boy looking for after-school snacks in the fridge?
To cover N's naked back when he sleeps?
To recover from Coltrane's *A Love Supreme*.

To recover alliance?
To recover the carpet, dismantling anthills of clothing.
To recover from a case of The Wine-Dark Seas.

*

Will someone ransack the shelves? Canine assurance, coins, thin leaves.

Remember: N introduces me to H.D. & Deleuze, to riding a bike as an adult, to multiple orgasms, to broccoli rabe sandwiches & homemade sauerkraut.

*

A "no touching" rule at the hospital. Afraid visitors smuggle in drugs or weapons. The nice nurses let N & I hug, touch each other's arms as we play Scrabble. "You can't touch," says the mean nurse, watching us separate before swishing down the corridor. Try not to cry. Rules betray need. Shifts end.

Faith: I stay busy with distant friends & packages. Fill glass vials with white beans, maroon ribbon, miniature books, a red tricycle. Cork. Bike to the post office. Only service dogs allowed inside.

Unfaithful: N asks me to scrape out the bowls & plates more thoroughly before stashing them

in the sink. To prevent drain-clogging. In return
I think, *I had to throw out your noose.* Of course
we don't want to clog our drains with oatmeal &
black-eyed peas.

N's shrink calls me back. Question medications. 10
months & I doubt his nurse practitioner who dubs
N "treatment resistant." What could that mean?
Higher dose? A different kind? Prescription bot-
tles line the butcher-block like rooks, I sponge
around them, toss out lost cashews. I say to his
shrink, *this is the only life he has.* I used to say this
about myself, detached from meds, as in, atheism,
as in, don't laze.

*

Questions I can't ask: Which parking garage were
you trying to jump from? Why where you listening
to Coltrane, to convince you to jump or to con-
vince you to stay? Did you say goodbye to our dog?
How could I be better off without you? What did you
think would happen to me?

*

Remember: N tenderly soaps my armpits in the
shower.

*

A bowl of coins lunges for the sun & an unseen squirrel steals tomatoes. Do I live the way I read? The you's face blurs, a sandcastle blown into the sea by a greedy umbrella. A bellow. Will someone clutch the outside lung? To hum into a bird's belly.

*

Therapy Session #7 Continued:

Dr: This may come across as pessimistic but maybe also useful: maybe when you're in the relationship, in the moment—& it's often this way for many of us—uncomfortable to be in full contact with what isn't okay. It creates a sense of dissonance that prevents us from fully understanding what isn't okay. When we have distance, it can be easier.

J: Right. Yeah.

Dr: What do you think about that?

J: I think that's part of the push & pull of how I'm feeling. I know all the concerns I have are more than the limit, but...

Dr: You said you're sad a lot of the time and that there are pieces that are missing, & that an aspect that's missing terrifies you.

J: But that aspect is also something that could theoretically be learned, which N is trying to learn. I think that's also what makes this so complicated: it's not like I'm in a relationship with someone who isn't aware of these things & who isn't trying to change. ALL of what he's trying to do is learn & change. My faith in him.

Dr: Yes. When you start to feel upset about certain pieces of the relationship that are missing, when you say to yourself, "he's working on these things," does it sit well with you? Or is it a kind of rationalization that has to do with moving away from what....is that what we were talking about earlier, about having the "incorrect feelings" & feeling guilty.

J: It's more that I can see him trying to change. I feel very sympathetic to this hard endeavor he's undertaking. It's exhausting for him, battling his history, his learned behavior, his daily suicidal thoughts. I don't feel like I'm using it as a device to keep myself optimistic or in this relationship. I genuinely believe he can make these changes. It's the timeframe—I know these changes will take a long time, & in the interim, it's really, really hard. For him, for me. I would need to either figure out a way to not be sad for the next five years or not to be accidentally collateral...I don't know.

Dr: Maybe part of the problem is that one never knows what someone else or even oneself will be like in five years. How far does that person have to move to be that person & what does that person mean to you, & how far would that take under ideal circumstances — five years is a figure, one year is another, 30 years is another.

J: Yes, 10 is another.

Dr: The fantasy of that person — it's a fantasy in that the person does not exist right now — who, really, that person is in the fantasy is something we need to get more clear about. In time it will be clearer whether this fantasy will become available to you.

J: Fantasy N.

Dr: Yes.

*

Ace Hardware also sells almonds & faucets.

Is there joy between us?

Remember: we play air-swim. N on the bed, holding my body naked & above, his hands levitate me as I pretend to swim, stroking the bedroom air. Sidestroke, breaststroke, I dive into his dry chest.

Skinnydip. Our dog barks at my ankles, trying to drag me to shore.

*

Faithful: This non-responsiveness, these three minute summaries of our days, this reading & grading in separate rooms, this avoidance of Feelings & Things Time, this automatic switching on of a movie as soon as dinner's served, I try not to take personally. Try not to see myself boring, flat, devoid, a receipt, a resurrection fern. Brittle.

Unfaithful: Drink coffee, check my email at Dazbog & then slyly cruise Craigslist for studios. I don't want to lose the library. To lose what I have faith in. I don't want lose-lose. That I write this, afraid to leave the document open on my computer? To feel a necessary secrecy.

Faithful: To believe the opposite of what N believes about himself: not a failure, not unfixable. To *not* wish for recovery, instead, to quietly wish N could accept his changes, these shiftings: how he can be sad in front of me, to unravel in the room, he lets me touch his leg. This, a new kind of uncovering.

Un/faithful:
J: I love you
but what are we doing?
N:

*

Will someone slap the light with mossy cheeks. A cut-up star. Reconcile to grief's thistled frock. Will someone hum when eating. The beehive waxes around a dog's bark. Will someone on the caved-in couch elect a broken feeling. Boxcutters. To leave the gift intact. O the baby's over there.

THE ACHE THE ACHE

My lilac hands. I know
you're breaking into an apple.
I can feel it. The overnight.
Clouds limp over swollen hills
as my freckles multiply, like how over-heated
bees litter the pavement.
I store my brain inside a straw hat.
I store my lust inside your finger.
The lists I store on paper. With two forks I whip
heavy cream in front of the window.
I listen to transportation more than
see it. I'm confused about who you are.
My wallet disintegrates, my lavender hair
I shove into your mouth, seal with
the flexing night. The thinnest pillow for
my breathy hibiscus. Can we pretend this
bathtub is a wave I'm trapped in? Its heat.
Can we not pretend at all? I drop diced fruit
into a bowl of sea foam.
Just tell me what you feel.

**

HAVE I BEEN REMOVED
FROM SOMETHING LARGER?

Boots leak & I can't find the comet after you call
its name. My body dents the roof of the van. From
now on I bike with my beak pointed to broken
glass. It's like cars are exploding into ice cubes &
sidewalk's the afterlife. I can only reference con-
temporary poems. My boots are too big, won't hold
up as muddy evidence on this hood. Ten trillion
strands of hair flare up like they have something to
cling to. Sometimes I don't want to locate my de-
rivative. Like a cane is hollow & filled with honey.
You twirl your hair into a vine. Swing from wind-
shield to the branch.

Babysitting money. Plastic cups. Pants cover boots,
get ground. A dark swing greets me. Crushes are a
safety thing. You run around the track backwards
like a heron diving into a pond. Surface victorious,
a fish for your lips. Dirt & glass & gravel socked
away. Like I come from somewhere. Like I founded
the Poetry Club. It's crazy that there's money.

*

These revolving domestic children,
initiates in the cruel.
A braided nest undoing my covers.
Feelings that you are separated.
The other guests.
Kiss me once.
Sorrow concerning something.
Sobs redoubling a moment.

*

I'm painting faces so they open. Matted hair, fallen pollen, a broken neck. Shredded stones shift in the blanket. Up in the van, too hot for subtext. Heat like a skillet. I sit in the iron sink. Bleach out the petals & paste on the hair. Little furrowed brow too thick for hospital corners.

The playground's off limits after dark, why we come here. Pour liquid into the night & then my mouth. Vans are good for lying on. We look up & run out of numbers. With a headlight moths take the spotlight. Pretend they're babies wavering on memory. Comets don't squeal. They fizz & their names pass by. We're derivatives. It's how I know to slam things down soft enough.

*

Flanked hill-breeze on which books
are buried.
The noble dust frosted the window.
Divided for a moment by an outside-gleam
about to vanish.
A walk in the sun & all the glorious
apses I've seen.
Flaming chimerical rain on money.

*

I scrape the driveway upon reentry. Gravel sprays
a syntax. The mailbox baptized in grief & the cur-
tains blush. I bring the pelts. Cold fur & a belt of
hot water for the underbelly. They coat the books.
They nest the text. Home is a gnat in the kitchen.
Let the dog catch it. Under the driveway, water-
bodies drone into fish form.

A looming. A list breaches in the summer shower.
A sideways. The face growing into the nose. I love.
In fleshy memory drying the dissolved didact. My
fingers through your belt loops. A rolled ankle &
clatter. Hot water. So long to the poem. The van of
non-love & dogs. I put myself back together in a
quarry. The part of you that's quartz. Dungeon of
moss & clean shirts like a manuscript's dedication.
Applying for the heart's foreclosure.

*

The marvelous independence of
the human gaze.
The moment pursuing,
like a beginning swimmer.
Intelligence objects randomly hurling.
Immediately I loved.
Heavy & vulgarized.

*

A mile from the see-saw. How my arms oar the wa-
ter & the light eddies outward. These are my deriv-
atives, my children of ghoulish glory running from
the cops. Opposite ends of the pond, we lose track
on purpose. Like a voyeur I'm the vapor. The Great
American Train Wreck is how we share the dino-
saur bones. So close to the water we smell iron
melt. High-beams show us who we are.

Hurtling towards the parking lot of a gas station.
Candy thieves tracking pollen with boots. Plastic
cups fill with quartz. Windshields covered in bug
guts. The van's hood is a hospital bed. I wrap a
Squeegee in a pink ribbon like a ponytail on the
first day of school.

*

The beak burned or boiled.
A comatose comet's your moth

caught between blanket & sheets.
I felt the onion in my eye.
I'm stuck with hibiscus in my hair.
Why do you care for doubles & fake children?

*

We write poems on the whiteboard of a cloud. Beginner swimmers in love with salty hair. I derive skipping stones to fling from my bike, a tent on the trampoline of text. You're my whodunit. I draw the liquid from any falling light.

A hand held head, name-calling. Ice cubes sounding in response. Do what I call you: pepper, smell like pepper. Honey, hurry me home. My noisy stimulus, a pox upon your forehead, your dripping snout, the pungent enclave of a cleft letter. Derivatives detonate like lemons in a van. All of the buckets, all of your heads. I've never been able to hold my breath that long. Who let me skip a grade.

WILL I DETECT THE AESTHETIC EXPERIENCE?

"I swim to shore every day"
— Elizabeth Willis

I drift through dirt like a minty tooth. A schooner loose on the eyelid shedding iambs. Where hints of birch burst open I wince at the deadpan panic.

I'm devising a device that detects. It's a feeling. The leaf I'll catch before it slaps the grass. "The movement by which air is made to enter the lungs." Made to?

Teething cumulous. Harmonics sprint along my side of the frequent daydream to dissuade those who stand so still for inclusion. Blasphemy an impossible draft. A face flanked by doubt & the curved interlocutor. Leafbound. Lying in the back of a pickup truck I curate clouds. Drop the guardrails, ferocious fluoride!

*

Who can pay attention the longest? So many songs come from the shower. Laminate leaves or clean out the drain, the grapes, the fury of its avenging families. Flies cling to memory like a cenotaph. Say aaaaah. Say ache.

Vesselling. I rip the fingers off my glove. To ply & to plaything. The sweeping sound of a bookcase push. Burning ballasts start like a rucksack levitating plums. End like an unstable current. My contrails. They streak in the language of whiteout that contributes without correction, leaks out & then quickly disappears. Shallots of disappointment.

Look up anyways: the afterhours of stars. It's a matter of what we want to sustain. Shape or sharp or hints of music in the sand. Fractal feelings to tendril.

*

Vigilant curiosity. A request without curtsy. Trochees clean the gums of worn-out brine & bristle. Ashing into attention. Horizon as anyface, air-pocked by syllable. I don't want to miss. This flight.

Look at a painting, dammit, look at a word: translation, the only enactment. Bilge or buoy, it will be godless. It will flip an image into feeling. The coquettish twins of relief & release.

"The movement by which air is expelled from the lungs." Which air? The non-lived coming to life uncontained by beauty. Leaf-splatter & my asphalt oven.

*

Is there something I cannot doubt? Is it debatable? A detour? Dirt? Floss or lean on your fist to prop up the face vigilant with weather. Restoration of the apparently drowned. The bathrobe's not alive but slumps whitely in the last place I clung. Something like short history I shore to feeling. An act that uncovers the shell pulped of my bloody sound.

Hold an ache. Smoke out the stutter for a honey-ride of sound. Briny book. Hold my ache, my stormy, my lamp-tooth, release my—

I act upon the air, I act upon the feeling. I'm a time capsule rustling in relief. Like the fractal shore, remain unmeasured.

ATTACHED TO THE SWAN COMES THE WATER

Are you willing to wake me with your baby? To trust I won't cut your luscious bangs as you rest?

My two children we send to the school best fitting personalities of orange sheets, newspapers smeared with coffee & glitter-recycling. Tin cans emptied of black-eyed peas & kale on the counter. Art-class kites are the chipped teeth of love.

Kids have regrets, which is the hardest thing to let them have.

Train yourself to hold your breath for the life of a mitochondrial high-rise. The nooks of our cement bookshelves nest uncapped pens & paperclips.

Hanging off the bed like a white seal, our dog's head watches the window for unsafe shapes. A foreign tail or ominous boot. Under three blankets I sleep, reject a space-heater. We're excavating the last light bulb. Yes, we do this. We share the same careless plants.

Leaf-eyes folding against fat glass. An ego dissolving in bathwater.

*

I want to build a house that tames worth & won't last. The light won't stop where we live, needles through the rafters & the gulp of. O we're not the pleats of wood so we last.

You're attracted to *me* or how you turn my body on? I'm afraid distinctions destroy me.

Our backyard licks up space like a sno-cone where we'll feed diamond-eyed goats. The house isn't afraid to die. Isn't afraid to ask for leg-rubs.

Cover me in a blanket too dirty to touch the face. My face loops around the park & the dog recognizes you as you bike by. Pulls me toward your spokes. I'm looking for a life like our own.

We'll train the goat to dig for broken egos of our unmeasured reciprocal. Exchange, the only endless lyric. So the gift won't die on wallpaper, wilt.

*

My dead phone, my neglected ice melting in sneakers & watch the rice cook for dinner. How reassuring the starch dribbles down & stains the pot. I feel you breathing when I hold the soapy sponge. I do.

A frozen tennis ball dissolves on our bed. This is not a metaphor for love, yet love, the dirt-freckled arm crossing rafters of children, is the plant spiraling from your bangs. Location, a choice. Attraction ripples out of my vase set on the coffee table.

*

Kites hide under the cover of kale. With questions & arms kids pinwheeling toward us. Tilted paintings nobody rights. The personality of our baby? Is physical, too? Domestic fantasies exist by the liter to unblur the future of shared space. A laundry pile of love poems. Your body like a warm moon.

Without abstraction. Without without the violent couch, violent vase, violent sink, O violent & matted rug. We'll empty the vacuum to the lyric stem, the vine that breaks the planter, water-swelling.

The backyard sways with antlers & baby teeth. Holding a dogbone graveyard, wriggle up the woodchip tree house. With latticed words lending the reciprocal bathtub.

Let's have a watering the plants date. A find the missing mitten date. An ice-cream in bed date. A talk date. The hot shower & how you soap my spine date. A how do you know me? date.

What are we, bystanders? With paintings slipping off the wall?

Talk, attraction, date. Sleepy meals? My attractive talk, like kite tails afraid of timing. Let's plant your luscious bangs in my chest.

I CANNOT NAME IT, IT LIVES

You are the splintered cloud of wood. Hum of halogen, a stutter strikes your microcosm's sharp connector-thorn. Home & the uncut call?

I'm laughing at blood. How can we judge the treatment of a corpse? How can we judge what has no antecedent? A generation should not repeat. Honey on the apple-slice, the fractured nature of speculation.

Object painted with asthma attacks. Object between relationships. Frozen object taken out of the freezer.

The wave of felt things, sprung & yanking down the intercepted rest. To forest spilt or catapulted light. Birdward, to the grumbling aggregate, girl.

A name, my betrayal. I let. A moderate proposal worn by paper cleft & left to paint the guilt. Abandoned, browned on your desk the leaflets sleep.

Object like a curator of dark trains in America. Object stinking up the gallery, an albino snake the artist forgot to cure. Objects abetting symbolic rituals like blood & barbershops.

Who calls it the apple of invention? I atomize the comb with muck & sighs. Having no god the self emerges.

Recording clean the broken bird of lies jostled to clot the clouds & spindle home. A truce I call the swarm that underlies the porch. The collar strains to capsize bone. When waiting crushed the blossom thick with wet hair, terror hits the teething, green flung arm. Desire fractures by name.

Object of another naked forest. Object of loss or glossy carpools. At fleeting generosity, object winking riptides, speedy critics.

The self negotiates language. The poem, a sound. Rings. Your light-switch of cracked mast. O skull of tarns of washed poetic doubt. So what. So promise, promise.

Painted what you call the shadow, cast the shadow you uncut. Did I betray the page? Not preventative, yet, in a million ways I'm here. In tiny, silent events.

Object of the lawless poacher, the wounded visual uncertainty. Object coaxing another object. In open-air, the object like a broken stair with teethy splinters & pink ankle.

Rent, coal, oil, soap, uncoil in the debris I manage to eat.

To pocket the safety leaf, the debt that carries ghostly my regret alarmed. A shock of violet kites, a stubborn mass to fight the birds for havocked air. Pull back to arm the blossom's bud. Skin slouches in the sun of names.

Object inside of movement. Objects fear endnotes & dry dog food. Object befitting the stranded sea. Home?

The density of a word, its cellular level I poke intricately awake. Indigenous to repetition. Your full-sink & floating asparagus tips.

Do not let the name, the name so young, into that home address of motionless bread. Flies at the end of summer nip at the bulked-up garden, compost raising like your sternum.

Object, are you lonely? Are you neutralized? Domestic? Perpendicular to my pose? Object too polite to expose itself. The object of movement. Object electrified.

47

Come here, apple, apple apple. I'll rent you a porch to weather your name. A page like a wave. Beach-front property. Open your repetitive window to air out the cushions. Sink of salty forks I drown with fists.

A letting. Let's hang out & felt the word into textile. Apply heat & moisture inside the halogen hummingbird.

Object ripe & nervous like a gnat-surrounded peach. Harelipped object. Object, did you eureka?

The name rends a sculpture of a girl, a girl with hands on her hips. Runs wifelike, wifeless.

Flexing with hybrid vigor. I'm inside a helix. History entwines like an alarm-clock hiccup. I betrayed my doubt with ease. Liquid paint & splinters of your make-shift face: on a coal train the self perches like a thorn.

Objects only materialize for those who call to them. Defected object. Objects bloody the bird with gym balls, recycled envelopes, lawsuits. Liquid face of your page.

THE ACHE THE ACHE

We think the sea is invulnerable & we are
wrong. I watch water evaporate from
the vase. I watch your face as it turns to water.
Cars are louder than I am. Above the street I am
staring at two green shelves leaning against my wall.
Like a sailor, I whittled my heart into a hook & threw
it in the sea. The sea is a sink, a ceramic duck,
your stack of paper plates saved for picnics.
Our dog whines & I don't know why. I've failed
in some way that has yet to be revealed.
Replace my heart with a lightbulb, a bleacher.
Nothing fits. I replace my heart with your
face. Scallops hold my hand, lead me to
that wet, grey scale. From the raft, I will the shelves
onto the wall. I will your face to look up
at me, from inside my chest.
Have I failed the sea. Refill the vase.

* * *

I WAS NOT BORN

I was made on the counter, tall as a vase. Smearing the window, watching my parents drive to the hospital. I'm waving.

Bring me back a sibling. A good one.

Bring me back something warm that stares. With its own blanket & cap. Smaller than a doll. Needles & a nurse stashing candy in the freezer.

I am the oldest, smoldering in a crib. What won't I outgrow? Why is my hair so thick? I hate bangs, they close off the opera face.

Let me burp you, let me show you the swamp. Let me toss a crabapple at your baseball bat. Let's take a bath together. Let's drink the sprinkler. Let's give you the rectangular room & a wooden sword & all the dumb names for hamsters.

Let's drive your toy trucks off the road. I was never born, I've had hair for centuries. You're on my side, see.

I scream a bit. I fill my pillowcase with canned food. I stare at a painting. Pastels. I live in a shell on the mantel. My finger finds a tunnel through the clay. I drip a castle onto the beach & an army of crab legs crown.

Jar the crab legs. Jar the white stones. Jar the chrysalis but punch holes through the lid. Jar the sparklers into smoke. Jar my cough. Give me back a pulse. Give me back my pile of paper. My clothing, clean hair. I'm sitting on the stairwell in sickness, in pale face, in fragile gown, listening to dinner clink below. I drink juice, swallow ten pills at a time. I was taught to fight this body & no one shows me how to stop.

Throw clay at the wall. Dip bird skeletons in slip & stick them in the kiln. A mother's maiden name, little feminist, don't like boys back. But I sleep in their tents, play battleship in their attics. Walk around with those I love like they don't have hands.

Paint the window with me. Wake before me & swim to the sea. Shake that salt on my pillow. I take books in the bathtub. I dunk books & they dry like waves. My soapy soapy hands.

What my body does has no name, has betrayed me. The needles the bottles the popsicles. What do little alveoli say? They speak when they want to. I'm a file, ten feet long of test results.

Test negative for leukemia, test negative for cystic fibrosis, test negative for mononucleosis, test negative for HIV. Whatever the next test is, if positive, I'll have a name. To call. Out of bed. I'm nine, give a class presentation on Ohio before summer breaks with pollen.

The shock of clumped hair in the drain. I have trouble asking for what I want. Hold my wrists. Don't doctor. Wring out these waterlogged limbs. Let me outlive my pet.

Some kind of ancient history: shake your head back & forth to kill the animal. How many children can we fit? The last one asks a parent for help. Extra toothbrushes, floss, pill bottle buds, & nail clippers on the shelf. We clip the flowers together.

Grief is a thing we store in a hatbox. It reads us stories of witches buying groceries. It has two stone lions & a broken leg. It has a collection of canes I get to keep.

O little jar of thorns, the thumbs rejoice. Arrange the flowers. I cut my sibling's hair, he shakes his head with a new neck. Air-neck like a buff tusk. The wooden sword he stabs the door with, I lean against on the other side. O damsel in distress, what maiden name

to pin thy chest. When the sword splits we use its limbs for kindling. I turn the animal over the spit. I wipe the shelf with the sleeve of my thorn.

So gone.

Two attics connect through a passage.

Flashlights & hands & knees.

The stuffing of a house falling out, among dead mice, nails.

To travel from one black O to the other is a rite.

To be nine & dusty, the leader.

The ignorer of spiders. I'm healthy & dead in this century.

I have no last words, only glances as I swallow the bird.

Everybird. The chimney brings.

Levitate me with your hollow bones.

Whatever ails you shakes the hand. Heat is a sibling. When the day happens you are watching a ripped piece of paper reveal a flagging ship. Siblings disembark full of water & glass. Ailments circle the idea sitting in the very same glass. As though it's going to show you something. On a particle level, sound is a pond that surrounds you.

When they come, they offer the rest. Coughs encased in the luxury of tutors & private school. I'm a pretend face between mast & bow. I dust the best thing. Your sibling is beautiful.

The body in feathers, the body in salt. I climb out of it with a flag for the sick & enough.

Brain-fog. My lungs call me the Sleep-Mobile. In autumn the bed in spring the hammock.

If my body takes away my brain. If papers scatter on the carpet then a deadline's passed. Then fight the mother instead of the doctor. How easy to fight her instead. Hide pills in the planters.

Sickness takes a certain kind of patience. To get thy brain back, little feminist, the weather must change. So I wait with her last name inside me.

If the letters are sewn into my sailor's cuff. If my gender's assigned a bunkmate. My hair ambiguous & shorn.

Where's my sibling? Home & I'm not forgotten.

The hammock is a leaky ship.

Let her name inflate you.

If you have patience, jar it.

I can wait for the right hand to hold.

To recline is to wait. O limp lungs.

A family shopping for my favorite foods. A family jars patience with me in the kitchen.

I cannot know what I'm missing.

Outtakes of health: Trampoline, pop-quiz, a soccer field, an essay. Hiking until the trees shrink to our knees. No symptoms near the lemonade stand & Dixie cups.

Little sibling let's roll our eyes. Let's eat Oreos.

Put the frog in the cookie-tin to scare the parents. We're a family in a canoe. Engaged with oars & shoreline.

For lunch let's swim to the raft with sandwiches held above our heads.

Do you miss the sickness? How to trust a body that's betrayed you. No cure if there is no name & there is no name for the cureless. So how could I hear you calling? A hairbrush melting on the lamp, a nap.

When to be healthy is to be another person.

Bones made of paper, scrolled tight & tied by a thin blue vein. Ringed as a tree revealing years. Maybe this is the trick: carve nothing in stone. Set snow or creases in beeswax. Not to say take these as hiccups, but trails slashed or waded out.

How to let you love this body that has betrayed me that I am learning to love for the name it holds.

In every doctor's office, a fish tank.

A fact so far away. Forgive yourself, I'm standing.
I'm not ambiguous I'm your daughter. Not fragile,
not reclining. I ignore the seasons like my sibling.
Let's find the hamsters' graves under the geranium.

My maiden voyage is a drunk ship blinding back
the lighthouse. Hi, my hair is certain & complete.
Like any other century.

When the sickness hadn't swarmed me.

I was sleepy & nothing more. I grieved for the nameless: O allergic shiner. O solitary juice & the pills expire. O card games bed-ridden & blameless.

I'll swim circles around you.

In the after.

I wear cute hoodies.

Do I have smooth cuticles?

I light candles with my fingertips.

A hue more beautiful than health:

I let you in the first time.

THE ACHE THE ACHE

The sexual darkness is no different
than any other darkness. Glowing
limbs, rustling & droplets, the hive's
motor. My computer tells me I've played
a particular song 97 times. Today
I accidently dressed like a sailor.
Today my heart's a spigot. We can't
turn off anything, really. Music is
a root system, clasps & we are shaken.
By I don't know what—a slow dance,
a leaf sinking in a pool, as car engines
shred illegible darkness, the lost coast.
What does breaching 100 mean.
I block the sun? Then the poem
shakes it free.

✳✳✳✳

THE BOOK IS NOT AN ARK

for LC

The back tire of my bicycle rolls away & the gear hangs like a greasy ribbon. This is the living. Books are not orphans.

Fangs swing to & fro, my tresses. My house moves on wheels & a tight face. It's three months pregnant, ready to talk & dog-friendly. Waters the windowed peonies. In the book of demented tennis, in the book of casual seashells, in the book dedicated to hijacked love & sun-blisters: all words are underlined, the sand underneath my face, cool like time.

Grapes shrink to raisins on the coffee table & new towels imprint fuzz along wet, visiting bodies. A miniature mailbox stands among the seedless. Books recording children sounding themselves out.

The neighbors & their band practice. Geraniums swerve so sturdy, invincible. I'm not the man perpetually succumbing. What is your password? Your password? What are your thumbs like? Strong in the manner of hallways, they press against the book's covers.

My tresses lose a bobby pin to foliage. It's okay to say uncertainty rocks me.

*

I strap skulls to my hands & amble, legs in the air. Crush leaves on the carpet. I like the thing we place things into. Do I open my eyes? Planting corn at midnight in the football field. Sonar, lonely—any standstill, fraudulent with starved history. Bones I clack over soil to harvest play like a leathered game.

Books cannot be coupled. Constellations prick distance into a feeling. Asymmetrical dishware sweating like sleepy silos. Some couples place stuffed birds on their bookshelves. Nests & decanters. My bicycle is a black plum of wet death.

If color is given to leaf. If clouds, too, exist through the night. Frozen rabbit? No, sugarbird sugarbird. Flowers light the ankles up. We layer language over space to give it shape. Gauzy with frontier. Don't remainder the feeling.

Only two pairs of everything? The reek of inbreeding is forgetful. What did your eyes spit out? What nobody wants to escape from. Accuse me of language. Or man-made extinction. Of all the ways to die, I know I'll never drown.

Children who read beneath sheets with flashlights. Sexed with language.

*

On the lake only words were on fire. What happened, the flower is anti-climactic? I don't think you get anywhere without feelings.

Chalkboard erasers slapping out words like a transparent train lost in the drinking fountain. That lake's rind could be wetter a fat lip eclipsing the teeth. Mimetic echoes flushed out of the underbrush. You thought recognition was a gift?

I return the swan to foam like spilt marrow. Tinfoil topping the candle. The heat of lint, crushed lip. Grab that fog! To swan. If the lampshade ships, off we go. Strange ice of affection. Language, a stand-in for feelings.

*

Every month I rotate books on my heirloom Bible stands. Cork lampshades & I don't own any Bibles.

On one, essays by Lisa Robertson, poems by Elizabeth Willis. On another, a busted camera, silver & black, split in two: the body & the flash.

When I dry my shoulders with terrycloth it churns my tresses into a terrible sound. I split the lake with my bicycle wheel.

A book is not a floatation device. A book is not perfecting your vinaigrette. Nor a liquid animal. Nor soaping your spine in the shower. Nor a lung transplant. Not an enemy either. Maybe a hospital. A tendency to change. This is the feeling.

Children who sneak into the jewelry drawer. Are the children who pretend to be parents. Now imagine language.

Only buy the largest towels. I don't understand what the rest are for. Towels should be cloud-capes, petite clouds not allowed. My bicycle handlebars are ram horns I'm afraid to flip over. Like a hot summer, faith stultifies language. Flaps about like torn moths. To bat against the lit screen with all that night behind you?

*

The plants in my shower slowly die. A dent in my straw hat.

I want to lurk in the gutter of language. Where children fish with bent bike spokes for paper-boats, keys, bottle-caps, the reek of living: games. A book-like residuum.

If I die in the air is my death domestic? I feel like a different kind of person with long tresses. More languorous, less mysteriously feathered. My posture should recalculate. What is a minor gaze? Violent like any clangor. Luscious. Beyond yellow.

A book cannot abandon. A book is not an egg or is it. A book of gravitation. A book of face. Of immensity. Of doomed laundry. Iris clocks & silt-clad soldiers. Of the ravished public. Of ruins & inceptions. Of untamed. To alter in recognition. Culverts.

*

My password: monstercake. My safe word: starfish. My favorite word: spoon. My most played song, "Boxcar" by Shovels & Rope, 120 times. My least favorite traits: too many sentences begin with "Umm," I have to drink to dance, tone deaf, anxiety, insecurity/timidity, have trouble talking about sex with the person I'm having sex with, though chat candidly with friends. In language what is the remainder? Can you feel it. The living & the sloughing of—

What is a minor person? Succumb to language.
Like water. Easy eye. I slow-danced with language.
Like the mighty mitochondria. To receive without
passivity.

It's okay to say you feel feelings until you don't feel
them. A book is a sluicing condition. Faith of the
face's night, of language's bloody constellations.

MERCY:
AN ESSAY ON VARIOUS TOUCHING

Curious drift. Your book of implacable petals turns, peering. Live cake like immediate lilies: we are to discover: so a letter-filled vial. "Roll the towel under the door to block the light." No discrete language. Nocturnal water ails like an anklet. Radiant gauge. Lily of a different angle. A drafty child, months of crisis. Literate chlorophyll as tincture?

For example, linguistic injury.
For example, a pepper-tin empty of spark.

Climb through the letters. Shopping cart of lettuce, roots twisting to shake your hand. Clasp & turn away. I'm no longer afraid to crackle on your record player. Diamond nose, pecking. "Is it there or isn't it?" My own guess. My tooth-book. My swerve-book. My schoolboy exercise stamped with nostalgia. "Why weren't you going to leave a note?"

I dissect the leaves & keep the veins. Language does not give up.

For example, horary pillows.
For example, I pummel your lips.

Syrup on porcelain, a castle built from crusts of bread. As an infant I revolved around a nipple & the wooden slats of sleep. I revolved around the pattern of doodles by the phone. Downstairs' voices. Doctors' bills. Language pulled like taffy to gum, to holster. I resolve to do a jig, to laugh a little. My legs bridge over your lap like a decade. Can a thigh fill the gap?

For example, it's no-bra Sunday.
For example, I smell the frying pan on fire.

Language gives up your body. Mercy. Lightning bounces back toward your face, parted & watering plants. Myth pearled into a pierced being I strung & flung into an avian nest, out of sight, bristles, lies. Last fall's doll we find in the snow-melt. "What is killer chocolate?" A fear barely flicked. I'm a hull, a hood, your glance declawing the hyacinth's breeze. Brim curious.

For example, this is a love poem to the poem.
For example, a love poem to you, confused by fear.

I was wrong when I wanted to count how many
ways to stay warm. Not warmth at all, the touch of.
How many ways in place of distance. Whatever it is
your teeth do to my ear. Planting words among the
wild flowers like frosting. "Discard the shell & the
haze." Shredding napkins. "Can you interpret this
rigorous light?" The river wrinkles like text or touch.

For example, a dog in a nest of sweatshirts.
For example, sticks we throw in the sunken garden.

I think your language came out to touch me. Bent,
diaphanous, wet. Drop the gavel into that liquid
vial. Applebreath let's swim with the lilies. Les-
son in a stitched-together speech. Scarcely count-
ing, entirely age. Straws swept daily. Information
shoots through with textual economy, natural, ob-
vious, contrary. If we rip the towel away: light un-
leashes. Stars, finally.

For example, hooray!
For example, everyone's defenses equal events.

From the gut a shadow sprung. Vowels. Dishes stacked to remind us of context. Your book bifurcated by my hands. A book equal to— Between swing & swallow. Between imagination & the act that follows with leafless ease. "Rip my clothes off?" Give yourself up, reverse erosion. Lilied river around the cake. Axing the nocturnal page or your caesura's bent lip. If I fog the vase from the inside, am I anxiety, lightning, chlorophyll, touch?

For example, homemade haircuts.
For example, an anxious refrain severed from song.

Soap-nest bubbles up. List of hair, distance, children linking arms, tall weeds we hide in. For the gravel in the yard, dissolve your teeth like corn. "Share text." The kitchen above ours seeps into the metal sink. Slackened sibilance stirring the petulant, measurable accident. A despair I don't want to open like illiterate lilies. For example, long distance is language. Mercy, diamond, mercy.

TO SUSTAIN IT

I peel garlic. I hate peeing in the dark like after
our electric fire, the brief life of the barefoot,
when I thought I was brave. I'll bear you flowers
& vegetable broth. I use knuckles to eat slower
in war. I'm trying to create a sincerity I can live
with, which is not an obligation of the poem.
Who trained you as anti-window? To look at me
as though accused, as though I called you on
it. To surround "for now" with a bereft arm. Or
water.

*

We throw eggs from my balcony: if the instinct is
the poem, if the human aggregation, if we sleep on
the balcony, if detritus made luminous collects, if
underneath the tablecloth canopy, if soap in your
scalp, if I count 47 train cars, if reacquainted with
objects, if brown bread & brown rice for summer,
if operating through mood & loss, if we all fit in the
bathtub, if an intricate pooling, if layered fractures

of sense, if I lie on white carpets to speak on the phone, if the eggs reach the sea, if the threat,

*

Half of war is water you bequeath to the houseboat. You leave chance to water. Garlic bobs around my head. Leave me & the squirm of my wake bends the pink-knuckled grass. I trust the fat of the mud, the beady eggs bubbling up against my thigh. Trust is black silk, the grass of the green worried night. "Is that a real poem or did you write it yourself?" To inform is to give shape, O not even the fragment stands alone.

*

We open windows to fade the paintings: if mood-based logic, if an apron & nothing underneath, if the fold-out couch contorts, if our instincts are selfish?, if the dry walk from the train, if I fall over, if I fall between rocks into the sea, if the Astro-turf slips off the balcony, if I don't know what to do with your sex parts, if we roll the tree-stump into the elevator, if the threat is our instinct?, if more pooling, if writing erased?, if you could hear the parentheses fail to close,

*

The moon disease. The moon cannot smell or flame or canteen. I cart my knuckles to market at midnight. Vowels come out of fire like how in my watery house the cutting board reeks. Repetition in poetry is resistance. Don't eat eyelashes & wreck your appetite. Form is a plaything, an extruder, an active: four sandals that weigh the beach blanket to the sand & the sea-wind that buoys any corner. I watch what flaps to shift the lid. I flock, finger, deform the lingering.

*

The paycheck we glide on: if I mildew your laundry, if I crack the ice-cube tray, if the blanket's on the balcony, if the egg hits the tracks, if your bath alarms, if we lace fatty moods to the poem, if the instinct defeats me, or, if the instinct defies the white carpet, if the soapy bowl dries, if curtains sustain the painting of a balcony above war, if I can't look like you, if body parts rain from the elevated train, if all my prayers are threats, if the mood pools into a sense of eggs, if we run out we throw spare-ribs, if the poem threatens, if grass slicks the sea,

*

Carry my knuckles in the black velvet sack of a poem because it bends. I'll bear one female flower & one male & the poem wakes in the middle of the

81

moon. Sincerity is a kite, quiet, of alinear sex parts. Accuse me. Of curdled pollen & garlic sense. Of gripping a penny-filled sock. Of the poem's obligation to move. Elastic, foaming, windy, away from the general. Seat yourself next to a stranger & syntax shunts the messy desk of war.

THE ACHE THE ACHE

The split hairs of lightning, you
know how it goes: a peek, a point
of view, you fall over. Dust the lungs
for a release of lanterns. A centrifugal baby
or banshee in a shopping cart. Somehow
we're here to open up. Between library pencils
& a cabin of flush cosmos. Summer screens
grate the rain. Nice bicycle-boat. I want to
avoid something like the allure of that
golf course green & then the toxic ticking sprinklers.
I'll greet you with a smoking umbrella, wishful.
An open vowel. I skim regret from the lake, fling it
through the tire-swing so nothing stains.
My dress is soaked, like your handlebars are
meant to hold me up
against all the falling apple heirs.

*****

A YEAR TO THE DAY:
ON COLTRANE'S *A LOVE SUPREME*

"All gladness, dear Nelly, all light!"
—Paul Celan, entire last letter
to Nelly Sachs before suicide

I'm a lilac thief. For the blue vase in my new living room, for the clear vase on the nightstand in my new bedroom. At dark I stalk the avenues with scissors. Culling my neighbors' clippings. How I get here: a constellation of leaves. Against white paint. An impossible face.

The frozen river of you. Something human under eyelashes. 36 days we've lived a block apart. For 36 days I wonder if you've returned home each evening or if the apartment's empty, your public body hanging or smashed. I never thought a boxcutter could break my heart: in the shower together I notice & say, "Where did those scratches come from?" Our friends don't own cats. You say, "I wanted to know what it felt like." What does that mean. Yet your line breaks / are so emotional.

II months into your therapy & medication, I take a course on Levinas to understand what you believe. I think you forgot that while you're responsible for all others, they are responsible for you too. You have to offer the little o's of your Other. Even if the uppercase O is perpetually a leaf out of reach, high-shelved. With cloud.

*

You grew the biggest toe. I wrapped my whole hand around that one toe. A buoy, roadblock, a secret. This is how privacy turns into relation. Then relation turns to a series of memories.

In an apartment for one, all shoes the same size.

Two dried roses, snakeskin, scraps of paper flame in the traveling caldron. An inauguration like a key sewn to a palm-sized blank page. Red twine.

To crave a palpable response. Yet, I received scrim-shaw: etched, unwavering, detached. Severed tusk of love. I'm ready. I think I'm ready. I think, *I'm ready*. For what, for what I want.

I chant to myself: So little o so little o so little o so. So little o so little o so little o so. So little o so little o so. So little, o! So, little o. So little. o. Nothing I make is alive?

The anniversary of your failure to jump, & then your failure to hang. "Too many bikers passing by the bridge." Is that why? No day without fiction.

Given answers I didn't know how to question, I dead-ended. Petal-eddies on the pavement. You weaned language.

A brown carpet desires blue chairs. Take a photograph of the empty birdcage shadow on my wall. So who wants to see my replica of a shadow gliding a wall?

*

Therapy Session #13:

Dr: So a lot has happened since we last saw each other.

J: Yes, I'm a block & a half from where I was living before. It's been hectic & horrible, but it's starting to feel different.

Dr: Okay, so tell me more.

J: What part?! Last week I was just really sad: us living together yet knowing that there was an end to our relationship. Me, scrambling around trying to find a new place to live as soon as possible. At the same time, I don't feel that there is any animosity toward each other so it wasn't like hostile silence while living in the same place. It was us going about what we normally do, but much, much sadder. I feel tired from it all. It seems strange after five years of being together all the time, now we don't speak. It's totally gone. I guess that's what happens, yet it seems so strange. I'm losing the person I love the most.

Dr: Yes.

J: I'm adjusting to not having N in my life anymore; trying not to feel frustrated that a particular shared life you can put so much effort into just vanishes. The manifestation of it vanishes, not the history or experiences.

Dr: So it's sad & odd to be without something & someone that has been central to your whole existence for so long.

J: Yeah, on many levels. Our days were incredibly intertwined. I also feel like his health & the future of our relationship have been the foci of my attention consistently for the last two years—it's weird to not, I don't know, to not have that anymore as to where my concentration & attention goes.

Dr: Right, a close relationship for five years becomes an organizing principle.

*

Your texts I can't yet delete from my phone: "I love you & your face." "I miss you. You're the violin of my string quartet." "If you were a flower I'd bang a flower." "Everything is for you. Forever." "I love you. Sit on my face!"

Suicide-desire is the rejection of desire for the Other's little o's. So, o? So little. Suicide-desire is the rejection of the worth in your own little o's. Rejects the accumulation of worth. Accepts all little o's as demarcations of failure.

I recognized your face, but you wouldn't let me read it. Or, it could not be read.

I crave oatmeal every morning. No one to scrutinize the bowl that looks like slop: ½ cup oatmeal, a handful of cashews, nutritional yeast, ground flax seed, salsa, two eggs. I'm full & ready.

11 months ago, after your release from the hospital, you only read Celan. All the poems & letters. What does this mean? I couldn't ask & I couldn't read along.

Finally today I check *Paul Celan & Nelly Sachs: Correspondence* out from the library. The intro quotes Celan: "Reachable, near & not lost, there remained amid the losses this one thing: language. It, the language, remained, not lost, yes in spite of everything. But it has to pass through its own answerlessness, pass through frightful muting, pass

through the thousand darknesses of deathbring-
ing speech."

Light from my new window wakes me at six a.m. ev-
eryday. In apparitions of light, I never hit the snooze
button. I'm the only one who waters these plants.

I pretend the wall-to-wall brown carpet is the for-
est floor, the dirt, oak leaves, & pine needles of New
England. As a kid, I asked my parents if I could
cover my bedroom in sand, to pretend I lived on a
beach. "I'll keep it in my room, I promise." Planned
to trade my bed for a hammock. I didn't believe my
Mom when she said, "That's not how sand works."

I packed only two summer quilts. For the first
three weeks the nights unleash a starry chill & I
sleep with slippers on, my hoodie pulled over my
head like a glowworm.

I catalogue the scents of the bodies I've slept
with: warm milk, hay, lilacs, clover, wet pavement,
almonds, lavender, lavender. You said I was black
pepper. Who could be clay?

*

Therapy Session #13 Continued:

Dr: We don't have to talk about this, but it's sort of
related. Maybe you'd be comfortable talking about

your decision not to come to your appointment with me last week.

J: I just felt like I was being sad enough on my own. I was fine with my own emotions & thinking through everything that had transpired. I didn't feel like there would be a huge difference between crying & thinking about things on my own or being in this office. I wanted to stay where I was.

Dr: Could there be a link between how sad you're feeling & not wanting to come here?

J: Yeah, that's what I'm saying. Not that I didn't want to be sad in front of you, but it was more like I was fine on my own, I didn't need mediation. I wanted to experience it firsthand by myself. Our appointment was scheduled only two days after we broke up.

Dr: It struck me that you said that you're feeling more busy than sad, & that felt good. I understand that feeling not sad is better than feeling sad, but...you're less comfortable feelings might get less room.

J: I mean, I think my feelings come out whenever they want to. You always see in movies when people cry on cue or at appropriate moments. But strange things catch me off guard. Yesterday I was texting N because I needed to figure out when to pick boxes up from his place. I received this flat response from him, which made me immensely sad. It was devoid of all affection or connection, it was devoid of the recognition that we knew each other in any significant way. It was strictly informational. Moments like that epitomize everything that's changing. So I don't feel like I'm busying myself & pushing things away. I've had one straight week of stressing out trying to sign a lease—my graduate stipend isn't enough to sign leases in Denver, so I needed to have my *younger* brother co-sign the lease with me & he lives in Atlanta—packing, being sad & being around someone incredibly sad. So, to me, emotions are very much present.

Dr: How do you feel like you're handling this experience?

J: Like I've been a giant mess, but that I'm a giant mess in private. Or, I've been with N. I don't really tend to fall apart in front of my friends.

Dr: Do you feel like you could fall apart here?

J: I think I've cried here before. I can't talk & cry at the same time—it's true! I don't know how people do it. So I guess crying seems more private because it's expressive but at the same time doesn't actually allow me to communicate other than the raw emotion — usually someone is waiting for a response of more than tears. But I was hanging out with my friend S who is best friends with N, & I was just sitting at her house crying. So it depends. As I said, when I'm telling my friends how I'm doing, I usually feel more together than the random moments when I'm by myself & something unexpected triggers the sadness.

Dr: Struggling with conflicted feelings of what to do about this relationship was very central to what brought you here, in addition to anxiety disorder. You've been working hard to sort out different feelings you've had, what was & wasn't in this relationship, trying to anticipate the future of it. So you've canceled on our appointment during the most difficult week you've had.

J: I felt like I could be on my own.

Dr: How might that make sense?

J: I mean, because I've never done this before. Everything I've been going through is new. I wanted it to be unfiltered.

Dr: So in a way, you made an effort to protect your own experience of it. Is it possible, in that sense, it was useful to not come here. Because it kept you clearer about where you were?

J: Well, I felt like you'd ask me how it was going & I'd just cry. I was doing that on my own without any prompting. I didn't want to have to articulate what I was going through outside of actually living it.

Dr: So it could have been too much. That makes sense. You were using up enough energy having the experience, articulating it might have been a burden.

J: I don't even know if I could have, with the whole talking/crying divide.

Dr: In that sense, it was actually important that you didn't come. In terms of processing. You had to manage the experience. You've spent an immense amount of energy & time thinking about N's experience & where he is coming from.

J: I have all this extra time now.

*

Your face looked honest. Then fish-hooked like a false diploma. I think suicide is the desire to turn yourself into an object. To un-Other.

Where sprouts the distraction? I have to empty a room to fill the other with my body. Pay attention to every browning leaf.

It is tiring to keep someone else alive.

Accidently I rip the quilt. My hoodie's white cord hangs out of the antique bureau. Shadow-cars float on my wall's night. No one else can remember this for me.

Something empties from my brain. Makes room. For, is it lack of emotion or a calmness I'd forgotten?

Two dresses hang in the shower to steam. I'd rather have a surfboard than an ironing board. Try not to splash soap, to stain with what cleans.

My desktop has your folder named "N's Stuff." Inside, an article you started to write & never completed. You left it open last May & I read what stared at me, surfacing in front of my own documents. Did you mean to leave it open? I check to see if it's still in the folder:

"Somewhere between June & September of 2010, I'm not sure when exactly it was, I decided I was going to kill myself. One thing I wanted to do before I died was listen to *A Love Supreme* as many times as I could. I listened to it on vinyl, on CD, on iPod. I listened to it in the bath, on the train, while writing, while grading papers, while biking. I listened to it with other people. I listened to it alone.

On the morning of April second, 2011, I stood at the edge of a 16 story parking garage, watching the sunrise pink the foothills beyond Denver. The cold was still, present everywhere. The wind off the mountains chafed my cheeks. I sat on the edge of the building, looking out at the mountains, crying. In my headphones Coltrane's alto wailed. I looked at photos of Julia on my phone, thinking about how awful it was going to be for her...

John Coltrane was 38 when he recorded *A Love Supreme*. In short, I think it is the greatest piece of music of the 20th Century."

Unfinished, yet this is the moment I begin to hate Coltrane's *A Love Supreme*. I was the "other people." I was in the bath with you listening to this album. No day without fiction. I think: I soaped your legs in the tub, leaned against your chest. How those gestures drained into your suicide plan. "How awful it was going to be for her" to what? What, exactly? So little o. Your incompletion is my unending.

Nelly writes to Paul, "Despair / your letters like matches /spitting fire /No one gets to the end / but through the antlers of your words—"

Tulips look honest. I paint my toenails green for the stems & fingernails petal-red. Could I hide in a flowerbed. A face is never enough.

To know the o of your O. Ancestry of light. Re-member how you remember nights. I don't neces-sarily believe in walls, yet secretly want to design wallpaper. How much forgetting inhabits the decay of sadness. How much of you.

Your texts I can't yet delete from my phone: "Okay I love you. I'm going to rub & lick your pussy until you come 100 times tonight." "I love you." "I saw a cool pigeon." "Landed in Denver. Feeling sad. I miss you." "I love you for that." "That does not give you permission to eat him alive." "I love you. That's not from the story. That's science fact." "Landed! Safe! Fantasizing about licking your pussy til you moan & come." "Hello my blood, my bone, my heart." "Every disease is a musical problem." "The lights are lit."

Your privacy, I've lost it. I have 10 blank CDs left before I need to buy more. I need stamps & laun-dry detergent. No one else will replace these. Post-cards ready to mail.

I address the little o of the Other: So, little o. So? The opening of the opening. The violent light.

I collect scattered glasses through my house: two on the nightstand, one on the coffee table, one in the bathroom, one nesting the desk on a stack of papers. I wash them in the sink & hang them up-side-down in the dishwasher to dry.

You were my Saint of Lost Books. Not out of desire for neatness or organization I alphabetize my books: without a saint, titles dislocate. I have no memory for spines.

Sleep in tennis socks. Inevitably one slips off each night. In the morning I fish the bed like a bear in a lake, pawing for what I know is there.

Nelly writes, "Paul, dear Paul, your poems breathe with me day and night, and so they share my life."

How many times did you listen to *A Love Supreme?*

*

Therapy Session #13 Continued:

Dr: Maybe it was overwhelming to have this much of your own experience.

J: I mean, it's overwhelming in that everything is changing all at once. I feel that the experience of this week is pretty similar to when I had to bring N to the mental hospital. It doesn't feel that far away from what I was experiencing exactly one year ago plus three days. Although I was blindsided then; it's the same sense of overtakedness.

Dr: Were you feeling those feelings as much as you were right now? Because you were taking him to the hospital & managing *his* experience.

J: Yeah, I see what you mean, but for 10 days I was returning from visiting him at the hospital & crying & trying to sift through the disparate experiences of our life together. That was more of a shock. At least for this, I had my own warning.

Dr: Yes. I don't have a clear, articulated statement, more the sense that—perhaps in the relationship your emotions were more reactionary. N's difficulties emotionally took up a lot of the room. Even if he wasn't talking about it.

J: Right. I was still feeling things the whole time, but yes, I suppose they were more reactionary. Yes, now my emotions are the priority I suppose, or, that sounds narcissistic, maybe I mean, I am able to attend to them with more care.

Dr: You got short changed, *not* because he wasn't a good man, but because he was working on taking care of his own health & that has to come before taking care of someone else.

*

I water my herbs when I shower. Oregano with its

wily tentacles I haven't yet tossed in a meal. Mint's the tallest, a leaning & leafy Pisa. I've already replaced the basil. I take the hottest showers, a red stripe down my back. My new routine: I count slowly to 10 before stepping onto a turquoise mat, wash my face, brush teeth, stash the contact solution & comb back in the cabinet. I like to air-dry, to wash the dishes as the shower evaporates from my shoulders. Then I return to the bathroom & moisturize. Then clothing, pigtails, a single bobby pin.

Not yours, texts from others I cannot delete: "And it will be a full-size, hearse-shaped book with interior lights that you have to lie in, in order to read," "'Because we love them—all. That is the secret: a new sort of murder'—WCW" "I wish I had gotten off at your stop," "On that scale, it was small rabbit eating a snake," "What does AWOL mean?" "Parks. Sex. Bookstores. Sex. Cooking dinner together. Sex. Subway rides. Sex. Cocktails!" "Saw a book in a thrift store called *The Wine Dark Seas*. Not sure exactly what it was about. I didn't even pick it up & read the back. That's indicative of something," "I'm pregnant!" "In my dream last night you had two owls, each on a leash. I was in a wading pool."

Dear, esteemed Nelly Sachs!

I thank you, I thank you from my heart.

All the unanswerable questions in these dark days. This ghostly, mute not-yet, this even more ghostly and mute no-longer and once-again, and in between the unforeseeable, even tomorrow, even today.

Ever,

Your Paul Celan

I will find burnt corncobs. I will find seeds alluding starlings. I will find a lost daguerreotype, lost lipstick, a dry roof, smoke-bushes like rusted cotton candy. I will find accidents. Wind hiding the heat. Recycling in the trashcan & trash in the recycling bin. I will find someone sweeping water out of the potholes, over the asphalt canvas. Who can recover? Wind forgetting the light.

The volume of the vacuum cleaner scares me too. Is there such a thing as enough. Forget the parking lot's genus. Forget to look up the name of that bird. Forget you for a while. Lipstick left on the plastic straw. Have I already grieved? Under the new coffee table the dog cannot fit but he hasn't given up. I forget my chipped blue nail polish so much

darker than the sky. Count to 10 like it's Hide &
Seek & forget that no one's hiding.

*

Therapy Session #13 Continued:

J: I basically told him that I felt that he was doing
an amazing job of taking care of himself, & that I
could see all the progress—although I don't like
that particular word—advances, developments,
that he's made in therapy & medicine, reaching
out to friends, & the general day to day of tending
to oneself. But at the same time, that was a pri-
ority, & the second priority, which was our rela-
tionship, wasn't fitting into it well. Because he only
has time & room & focus for priority number one,
because it's so all-encompassing. I basically said I
loved him very much & had complete faith in the
changes he wants to make in himself, but that we
were in really different places with our lives & I
didn't know how to continue to reconcile that. The
circumstances created & carried a level of sadness
I couldn't fully dissipate.

Dr: It sounds like you were able to articulate your
love.

J: I was afraid I would change in a negative & irre-
coverable way. I've started to realize that I've been

expecting less, & that's made me give less, too. Even if N is healthy in a few years, I'm deeply fearful that I wouldn't even be the person he would love at that point, that my ebullience & my expectation for engagement would be too diminished. I was returning home at the end of the day no longer expecting someone to be happy to see me, & in turn, I was less enthusiastic. I don't want that for either of us.

Dr: So what happened?

J: We were both crying & incredibly sad. Breaking up was the worst-case scenario, basically. It sounds cliché, but I've fought harder then I ever have for anything to make this work & I didn't want it to end this way. It seemed like there was no other healthy alternative. So, we were just really, really sad. I got the sense that there was a big part of him that felt he was trying to heal & get healthy for *me*—which is not why he should be making the effort—but in those wine-dark sea moments, at least, thinking of being with me was the positive outcome. It was incredibly hard for him to hear me take myself out of that equation. I wanted to be there to help him get through this, too. I love him. Probably more than he could ever let himself feel. [Audible sigh]. So we talked on & off for a week & then I started moving into my new apartment on Saturday.

Dr: How are you feeling now?

J: Even though in some way I took control by ending the relationship, this wasn't what I wanted. It all seems strangely out of my hands. We have all the same friends, we go to the same events, we share the same intimate world. I could be capable of spending time with him in a group—not that it wouldn't be sad—but just that I'd rather have some connection than nothing, than total absence. I can think about ways of negotiating his presence so that it's better to have him in my life than not, because ultimately I'd like to think that after five years this doesn't end in silence. That might actually make me angry. I'd like to figure out a way for us to be friends in the long term, but again, it just feels out of my hands. It's what I want, but I might not get what I want because it all has to do with how N handles it. It's frustrating. & when he's healthy & with someone else, my heart will probably ache all over again.

Dr: Back to the same problem of waiting to react to someone else.

*

My insides of non-light. An absence referring to being. Language's accident. Bellicosity sounds gentle, without knuckle.

I buy green sheets. I buy five succulents, place the jade plant in the birdcage. I buy a vacuum cleaner. I buy a coffee table. I buy two shelves. I cry with a sadness that is never about one thing. It's that you're a block away. For you return home at night & I wouldn't know. For the names of our children, they pop like bubbles poked with a boxcutter. For the song about your love of sandwiches. Your song about my boots on the bed. For how you squeezed my neck at night. For how you squeezed the meat of my thumb while watching movies. How you curated our life with the record player.

So little o so little o so little o so. So little o so little o so little o so. So little o so little o so. So little, o! So, little o. So little. o. So o.

How many times did I listen to *A Love Supreme*?

My computer floats vocabulary words across the screen when it sleeps. The program's imperfect & often the same word circles the block like a stutter. Today, whenever I look up from my book, "major-domo" skates by. Dishwater drains from the sink when the disposal gargles.

Not yours, texts from others I cannot delete: "Punch the truth away," "You have an awesome voice!" "I read your text message in the middle of a dream. Buy two pairs of everything," "You are not a leper, but a leprechaun! A fancy lady one!" "You look like a tulip," "Baby is fine! I'm so happy I can't stop crying. A girl! Oh my my my my my." "'The written page is no mirror. To write is to confront an unknown face.' — Jabes" "An extremely drunk ship captain is trying to recruit me to apprentice on his boat."

*

Therapy Session #13 Continued:

J: I understand that I have this new space all to myself, & I'm trying to live in the calm of that space: the space of the actual experience, not the meta-analysis of the experience. Yet, he's still a part of my larger social world, which intersects with the calmer space I'm trying to create & maintain.

Dr: I wonder, if you feel angry about the idea that you might not be able to have a friendship with N because it's his decision, how you could think about it in a different way.

J: Well, although I feel a little like a bystander in regards to that situation, I know that possible friendship is about the long term, & what I *can* do is not obsessively think about wanting something in the distant future I can't control, & focus on what is immediately in my presence, that I can actually interact with & engage. I have a whole new life to build up now, I guess. Which is where my attention should be.

Dr: Yes.

J: But it felt like I was making the wrong decision. Because I love N with an intensity I'm grateful to be able to experience. I have faith in his ability to learn to care for himself. But I do feel calmer now. All the anxiety that has been consuming my thoughts has vanished. In its place is this quiet vacuum, where I can experience new routines, emotions, thoughts as they happen, instead of interrupting them with anxiety. I'm in them fully, time feels slower, more wrapped around me, fluid. I'm no longer waiting to see how someone else will react first. I don't know, but I think that's a good sign?

*

Lilac thievery ends by mid-May. I'm afraid of empty vases & fiction. My phone only holds 107 text messages & I've saved 103. My new stairwell is a frostbitten mauve. Where chipped, orange glances give warmth.

Nelly writes to Paul, "for the way in and way out / can never be the same…"

Try to remember: hold the memories that sustained these years without feeling crushed by the loss of a certain future.

A nest of scarves. Two quarters I save for laundry. A broken alarm clock, plugged in. This blue pillow-case now looks grey against the new green.

You can't keep someone else alive. But you can try. Everywhere it is face. Why is *A Love Supreme* the greatest piece of music of the 20th Century.

THE ACHE THE ACHE

for BZ

From inside the mountain I'm
a drum. Inside the drum, I'm
counting slowly to 10, trying to step
out of the hottest shower. Next
& naked, I wash the dishes to air-dry.
People leave by airplane. They leave
by UHaul. By cloudy Fords. With full
tanks. By noose & ash. I know they're not
leaving me, per say, but how do you not
feel left. Silhouettes fill with pollen &
slivers of soap. Somewhere you're
eating breakfast or hanging from my mind's
bridge. Somewhere you're sidereal, fixing
high beams. Or blowing eyelashes from your
computer keyboard. Inside the mountain is
room temperature. Air circulates through
a series of words. I stack three towels
for guests. An new bar of soap for the squeamish.
Soon a silhouette will send a painting in the mail.
Of a bloody train, a lace carousel, the sound I'm trying

to fill each space with. Outside the mountain
my hair glints like a CD on your dashboard.
Transportation means I miss you. Or maybe
a mountain could find a tunnel. Like how right now
my arm plunges into your guts. You are a drum set.
The sky above these plains looks like it belongs
to the sea & here I am with these excited eyes.

******

THE ACHE THE ACHE

Are we all reading books waiting for
someone to talk to us? Splash me
with blood, with wings
of yellow jackets, with infested
lecterns. Books squish
the nectarine in my bag
& snack juices into extinction.
We're something else outside, inside
this whirring hour, the economy
of sound. Bees higher than pollen
could float. What is a research rut?
Or a break from studies? Turn over
the book. I remember the first person
I was afraid to love. Or rather,
how-I-loved lost to the fear-of-sex-parts,
the uncontrolled. To manifest, yes.
I see through paper, leaves,
the face, to the back of your bold blood.
How the chalk on my hands
used to be words. I'm not afraid

to die, I just don't want to yet.
Ice-cream & grass stains belong
to children. A book props my head
above the green & its drafty prongs. Once
I was afraid of judgment & now I'm not.
Nothing belongs unless we want it to.
The ache, the ache, the ache, yes sonically.
Sear fruit to our blood, gasp & gasp back.
I see bees high-fiving leaves.

THE ACHE THE ACHE

for Nelly Sachs

To send paper boats to your sink.

Books are not orphans.

To swim out of the coffin.

My eye-lid raised.

To pinch a cloud through the window.

Crystalline letters, fever.

A capsized ache, to look.

Polar light.

To look at your wet—

THE ACHE THE ACHE

Maroon lint from the dryer makes me
wonder what I wear. Dog's leash
sprawled on the carpet & a bereft beer opened & left
out overnight. I have an irrational fear of
venereal disease. Like, I'm standing in the street's puddle
& something insidious springs from damp ankles.
To grind in the disposal woeful egg shells & onion skin.
Sometimes I'm afraid I want to get married
for the wedding & have children for the names.
If I tell you what I fear it's easier.
Fruit flies hover like lost freckles. A watermelon
hacked into rose quartz is what glimmers.
To wash & wring out words—they're not
cleaner or softer—they feel.
I'm marooned & recovered by language daily.
We've all swallowed a seed to see what would happen
or snapped an apple core into an hourglass.
In this ice-cube hour, I make myself visible.
Rent is a place for feelings. I open
the birdcage roof to water the plant.

I've never talked to the dead, though
I've prayed to a stuffed animal & a cloud:
Please let the plane land in one piece. Or, *please
let this work out between us*.
Something like a faith in pushing words
through the air? White dog hair on a grey sweater
reminds me not to care about certain outcomes.
How many times we have invented wings.
What words will you make? Swarming with seascape.
I'm looking for a breeze. Names squirm with
sticky melon children. The pull of letting. Now I mouth
Let this be okay. Look forward to watering plants.
Look forward to the ache of each word & how
they skip gleefully over the sea before sinking.
This is the new place for feelings. A wet castle grows
under the waves, it does not fear.

THE ACHE THE ACHE

The sea isn't even close.
I've learned that the face
is not enough. If you're the quarry
where is the cart of extractions?
To gather like an invitation.
An arbalest zings though quarreling trees.
Wind like a treaty cannot wait.
Sometimes the war warbles:
I will send you lavender & antimatter.
I will send you the splintered telephone.
I will send you a blamable cufflink.
I will send you cucumber moons.
The infinite stretch of a black hole
is nothing like me. Nothing like
the acute faith that unfreezes
the face's language. Had you flown
the quarantine flag in early light
what help could have—
what kind of help—
Sometimes I miss myself.

Sometimes I gather dead bees
in a soapy satchel.
Weather is whatever's there.
My blue blue veins, circling.
I have faith in you. It's my best
offer. My only offer. Twirl
a dirty curl with one hand & type
with the other that the forest holds.
Creativity is survival. I'm trying not to
miss myself anymore.
It has to do with feelings.
A few words ignite & signal biplanes
swooning through the chest.
Most only ash to anger, which these lilacs
extinguish. The sea is not wine-dark. It is lilacs.
My tresses, my tresses, mercy.
If you give a feeling away
then someone can help. Mortal kite,
the snap of an inchworm Crayon,
& letting it creep out of us.
Alleviation is a certain kind of space,
quavering. Unlike feelings, we cannot
eventually assuage language.
Ash caught in my blond. Out of bounds
of my green, your face. I'm not
trying to reach anything, I'm
reaching through it.

THE ACHE THE ACHE

Standing in a raggedy yard as Jen takes
photographs to send her sleeping boyfriend
we consider rent & location. We consider
biking in winter. Selah smells good today
& I tell her so, her kimono reminds me how
as a child I searched for an object
to make me unique. Is effortlessness a personality trait?
I tried a ring on each finger. I tried Billie Holiday.
I tried root-beer milk. Objects cannot do this.
Sommer is due August 30th & Farrah is having
a boy. In Turkey, Julie, mountainous with twins. I hear
baby Ione gurgle through the phone as I talk to her mother.
Frogs in kiddie pools will collect into temporary pets.
I don't own a couch anymore so my dog sits in the chair
next to me & suddenly it feels like a waiting room.
If you're with someone when they want to die then
you're a type of weather. As a gift my sibling replaces
my bicycle's stolen tire. My sibling with lighter tresses.
With no tonsils & faith in this country. I'm here because
I'm not ready to leave the feelings. Each feeling

a lung swelling like linens on the line's breeze. To let
the yard fill. Seth, Emily, Brian in Massachusetts
with the mussels & thin steeples—my feelings will visit.
Disclosures: I've read *The New Yorker* since
fourth grade which probably makes me a jerk; I'd twirl
my hair non-stop if I could; washing dishes
is the only chore I like; I choose the sea;
sometimes instead of conjuring the flower's design
I see its name in white reflective letters & blame
street signs in Denver; I break & lose sunglasses
because new weather crushes memory. Umbrellas, too.
The closest I get to anger is sadness. If we could
inhabit feelings more than spaces. Or, this space
starts a feeling I can carry somewhere else.
I vacuum before I leave. Coastal kinship &
milkweed for monarchs. Certain anxieties I seem
to welcome: let the gauge hit empty before refilling
the tank; wait for the due date to send
the electricity check; the tallest bookshelf tilts
precariously forward. That I will fail to
understand what I read. Driving my sibling
to the airport in a borrowed car we pass
Dahlia Street. I walk the perimeters of my apartment.
Who beheaded my camera? Do I remember
the names of all my teachers? What year was I
most confident? These words I say in my head
most often: magenta, faith, lilacs, Rachmaninoff, the sea.
I think the prairie is only good for

watching lightning bounce back
to the sky. I have buried objects
in a yard I do not want found. I'm trying
to react to myself. Above ground. To find
faith in language's failures. What is okay to cultivate?
Is art the only tangible object?
Weather does not hold feelings of its own.

ACKNOWLEDGMENTS

Immense gratitude to these journals for previously publishing my work:

Ampersand Review
   "Will I Detect the Aesthetic Experience?"
   "Have I Been Removed from Something Larger?"
Black Warrior Review
   "I Cannot Name It, It Lives"
Boston Review
   from the series "The Ache The Ache"
BOMB Online
   from the series "The Ache The Ache"
DIAGRAM
   "What Did Writing Erase?"
   "I Was Not Born"
Evening Will Come: a journal of poetics
   "To Sustain It"
Everyday Genius
   from the series "The Ache The Ache"

The Leveler
   from the series "The Ache The Ache"
Map Literary
   "Attached to the Swan Comes the Water"
Puerto Del Sol
   "Mercy: an essay on various touching"
VERSE
   "Of Recovery"

Thank you, entirely: Cynthia Arrieu-King, Sommer Browning, Robert J. Cataldo, Lisa Ciccarello, Arda Collins, Jennifer Denrow, Farrah Field, Brian Foley, Daniela Gesundheit, Jonathan Hamilton, HR Hegnauer, Christopher Kondrich, Seth Landman, J. Michael Martinez, Keith Newton, Emily Pettit, Bin Ramke, Katie Jean Shinkle, Sampson Starkweather, Mathias Svalina, Paige Taggart, Danielle Vogel, G.C. Waldrep, Jared White, Megan Whitman, Elizabeth Willis, Benh Zeitlin. Special thanks to Selah Saterstrom & Eleni Sikelianos, whose encouragement to experiment with the paragraph form made this book possible. And to my family, always.

ABOUT THE AUTHOR

Julia Cohen is the author of two collections of poetry, *Triggermoon Triggermoon* (Black Lawrence Press) and *Collateral Light* (Brooklyn Arts Press). Her essays and poems appear in journals like *jubilat*, *New American Writing*, *Kenyon Review* (KR Online), *Colorado Review*, *DIAGRAM*, and *Black Warrior Review*. She teaches and lives in Chicago.